What was that fuckin' password again?

Kay D Johnson

Johnson, Kay D
What was that fuckin' password again?

ISBN 978-1-989194-52-2 (pkb)

GoMe! Publishing

Since this book holds all your private and valuable information, please keep this book in a safe place at all times.

A

Website:
Email:
User Name:
Password:
Security Question/Hint
Notes:

Website:
Email:
User Name:
Password:
Security Question/Hint
Notes:

Website:
Email:
User Name:
Password:
Security Question/Hint
Notes:

A

Website:
Email:
User Name:
Password:
Security Question/Hint
Notes:

Website:
Email:
User Name:
Password:
Security Question/Hint
Notes:

Website:
Email:
User Name:
Password:
Security Question/Hint
Notes:

A

Website:
Email:
User Name:
Password:
Security Question/Hint
Notes:

Website:
Email:
User Name:
Password:
Security Question/Hint
Notes:

Website:
Email:
User Name:
Password:
Security Question/Hint
Notes:

A

Website:
Email:
User Name:
Password:

Security Question/Hint

Notes:

Website:
Email:
User Name:
Password:

Security Question/Hint

Notes:

User Name:
Password:

Security Question/Hint

Notes:

B

Website:
Email:
User Name:
Password:
Security Question/Hint
Notes:

Website:
Email:
User Name:
Password:
Security Question/Hint
Notes:

Website:
Email:
User Name:
Password:
Security Question/Hint
Notes:

B

Website:
Email:
User Name:
Password:
Security Question/Hint
Notes:

Website:
Email:
User Name:
Password:
Security Question/Hint
Notes:

Website:
Email:
User Name:
Password:
Security Question/Hint
Notes:

B

Website:
Email:
User Name:
Password:
Security Question/Hint
Notes:

Website:
Email:
User Name:
Password:
Security Question/Hint
Notes:

Website:
Email:
User Name:
Password:
Security Question/Hint
Notes:

B

Website:
Email:
User Name:
Password:
Security Question/Hint
Notes:

Website:
Email:
User Name:
Password:
Security Question/Hint
Notes:

Website:
Email:
User Name:
Password:
Security Question/Hint
Notes:

C

Website:
Email:
User Name:
Password:
Security Question/Hint
Notes:

Website:
Email:
User Name:
Password:
Security Question/Hint
Notes:

Website:
Email:
User Name:
Password:
Security Question/Hint
Notes:

C

Website:
Email:
User Name:
Password:
Security Question/Hint
Notes:

Website:
Email:
User Name:
Password:
Security Question/Hint
Notes:

Website:
Email:
User Name:
Password:
Security Question/Hint
Notes:

C

Website:
Email:
User Name:
Password:
Security Question/Hint
Notes:

Website:
Email:
User Name:
Password:
Security Question/Hint
Notes:

Website:
Email:
User Name:
Password:
Security Question/Hint
Notes:

C

Website:
Email:
User Name:
Password:
Security Question/Hint
Notes:

Website:
Email:
User Name:
Password:
Security Question/Hint
Notes:

Website:
Email:
User Name:
Password:
Security Question/Hint
Notes:

Website:
Email:
User Name:
Password:
Security Question/Hint
Notes:

Website:
Email:
User Name:
Password:
Security Question/Hint
Notes:

Website:
Email:
User Name:
Password:
Security Question/Hint
Notes:

D

Website:
Email:
User Name:
Password:
Security Question/Hint
Notes:

Website:
Email:
User Name:
Password:
Security Question/Hint
Notes:

Website:
Email:
User Name:
Password:
Security Question/Hint
Notes:

D

Website:
Email:
User Name:
Password:
Security Question/Hint
Notes:

Website:
Email:
User Name:
Password:
Security Question/Hint
Notes:

Website:
Email:
User Name:
Password:
Security Question/Hint
Notes:

D

Website:

Email:

User Name:

Password:

Security Question/Hint

Notes:

Website:

Email:

User Name:

Password:

Security Question/Hint

Notes:

Website:

Email:

User Name:

Password:

Security Question/Hint

Notes:

E

Website:
Email:
User Name:
Password:
Security Question/Hint
Notes:

Website:
Email:
User Name:
Password:
Security Question/Hint
Notes:

Website:
Email:
User Name:
Password:
Security Question/Hint
Notes:

E

Website:
Email:
User Name:
Password:

Security Question/Hint

Notes:

Website:
Email:
User Name:
Password:

Security Question/Hint

Notes:

Website:
Email:
User Name:
Password:

Security Question/Hint

Notes:

E

Website:
Email:
User Name:
Password:
Security Question/Hint
Notes:

Website:
Email:
User Name:
Password:
Security Question/Hint
Notes:

Website:
Email:
User Name:
Password:
Security Question/Hint
Notes:

E

Website:
Email:
User Name:
Password:
Security Question/Hint
Notes:

Website:
Email:
User Name:
Password:
Security Question/Hint
Notes:

Website:
Email:
User Name:
Password:
Security Question/Hint
Notes:

Website:
Email:
User Name:
Password:
Security Question/Hint
Notes:

F

Website:
Email:
User Name:
Password:
Security Question/Hint
Notes:

Website:
Email:
User Name:
Password:
Security Question/Hint
Notes:

F

Website:
Email:
User Name:
Password:
Security Question/Hint
Notes:

Website:
Email:
User Name:
Password:
Security Question/Hint
Notes:

Website:
Email:
User Name:
Password:
Security Question/Hint
Notes:

F

Website:
Email:
User Name:
Password:
Security Question/Hint
Notes:

Website:
Email:
User Name:
Password:
Security Question/Hint
Notes:

Website:
Email:
User Name:
Password:
Security Question/Hint
Notes:

F

Website:
Email:
User Name:
Password:
Security Question/Hint
Notes:

Website:
Email:
User Name:
Password:
Security Question/Hint
Notes:

Website:
Email:
User Name:
Password:
Security Question/Hint
Notes:

G

Website:
Email:
User Name:
Password:
Security Question/Hint
Notes:

Website:
Email:
User Name:
Password:
Security Question/Hint
Notes:

Website:
Email:
User Name:
Password:
Security Question/Hint
Notes:

G

Website:
Email:
User Name:
Password:

Security Question/Hint

Notes:

Website:
Email:
User Name:
Password:

Security Question/Hint

Notes:

Website:
Email:
User Name:
Password:

Security Question/Hint

Notes:

G

Website:
Email:
User Name:
Password:
Security Question/Hint
Notes:

Website:
Email:
User Name:
Password:
Security Question/Hint
Notes:

Website:
Email:
User Name:
Password:
Security Question/Hint
Notes:

G

Website:
Email:
User Name:
Password:

Security Question/Hint

Notes:

Website:
Email:
User Name:
Password:

Security Question/Hint

Notes:

Website:
Email:
User Name:
Password:

Security Question/Hint

Notes:

H

Website:
Email:
User Name:
Password:
Security Question/Hint
Notes:

Website:
Email:
User Name:
Password:
Security Question/Hint
Notes:

Website:
Email:
User Name:
Password:
Security Question/Hint
Notes:

H

Website:
Email:
User Name:
Password:
Security Question/Hint
Notes:

Website:
Email:
User Name:
Password:
Security Question/Hint
Notes:

Website:
Email:
User Name:
Password:
Security Question/Hint
Notes:

H

Website:
Email:
User Name:
Password:
Security Question/Hint
Notes:

Website:
Email:
User Name:
Password:
Security Question/Hint
Notes:

Website:
Email:
User Name:
Password:
Security Question/Hint
Notes:

H

Website:
Email:
User Name:
Password:
Security Question/Hint
Notes:

Website:
Email:
User Name:
Password:
Security Question/Hint
Notes:

Website:
Email:
User Name:
Password:
Security Question/Hint
Notes:

I

Website:
Email:
User Name:
Password:
Security Question/Hint
Notes:

Website:
Email:
User Name:
Password:
Security Question/Hint
Notes:

Website:
Email:
User Name:
Password:
Security Question/Hint
Notes:

I

Website:
Email:
User Name:
Password:
Security Question/Hint
Notes:

Website:
Email:
User Name:
Password:
Security Question/Hint
Notes:

Website:
Email:
User Name:
Password:
Security Question/Hint
Notes:

I

Website:
Email:
User Name:
Password:

Security Question/Hint

Notes:

Website:
Email:
User Name:
Password:

Security Question/Hint

Notes:

Website:
Email:
User Name:
Password:

Security Question/Hint

Notes:

I

Website:
Email:
User Name:
Password:
Security Question/Hint
Notes:

Website:
Email:
User Name:
Password:
Security Question/Hint
Notes:

Website:
Email:
User Name:
Password:
Security Question/Hint
Notes:

J

Website:
Email:
User Name:
Password:
Security Question/Hint
Notes:

Website:
Email:
User Name:
Password:
Security Question/Hint
Notes:

Website:
Email:
User Name:
Password:
Security Question/Hint
Notes:

J

Website:
Email:
User Name:
Password:
Security Question/Hint
Notes:

Website:
Email:
User Name:
Password:
Security Question/Hint
Notes:

Website:
Email:
User Name:
Password:
Security Question/Hint
Notes:

J

Website:
Email:
User Name:
Password:
Security Question/Hint
Notes:

Website:
Email:
User Name:
Password:
Security Question/Hint
Notes:

Website:
Email:
User Name:
Password:
Security Question/Hint
Notes:

J

Website:
Email:
User Name:
Password:
Security Question/Hint
Notes:

Website:
Email:
User Name:
Password:
Security Question/Hint
Notes:

Website:
Email:
User Name:
Password:
Security Question/Hint
Notes:

K

Website:
Email:
User Name:
Password:
Security Question/Hint
Notes:

Website:
Email:
User Name:
Password:
Security Question/Hint
Notes:

Website:
Email:
User Name:
Password:
Security Question/Hint
Notes:

K

Website:
Email:
User Name:
Password:
Security Question/Hint
Notes:

Website:
Email:
User Name:
Password:
Security Question/Hint
Notes:

Website:
Email:
User Name:
Password:
Security Question/Hint
Notes:

Website:
Email:
User Name:
Password:
Security Question/Hint
Notes:

Website:
Email:
User Name:
Password:
Security Question/Hint
Notes:

Website:
Email:
User Name:
Password:
Security Question/Hint
Notes:

K

Website:
Email:
User Name:
Password:
Security Question/Hint
Notes:

Website:
Email:
User Name:
Password:
Security Question/Hint
Notes:

Website:
Email:
User Name:
Password:
Security Question/Hint
Notes:

L

Website:
Email:
User Name:
Password:
Security Question/Hint
Notes:

Website:
Email:
User Name:
Password:
Security Question/Hint
Notes:

Website:
Email:
User Name:
Password:
Security Question/Hint
Notes:

L

Website:
Email:
User Name:
Password:
Security Question/Hint
Notes:

Website:
Email:
User Name:
Password:
Security Question/Hint
Notes:

Website:
Email:
User Name:
Password:
Security Question/Hint
Notes:

L

Website:
Email:
User Name:
Password:
Security Question/Hint
Notes:

Website:
Email:
User Name:
Password:
Security Question/Hint
Notes:

Website:
Email:
User Name:
Password:
Security Question/Hint
Notes:

L

Website:

Email:

User Name:

Password:

Security Question/Hint

Notes:

Website:

Email:

User Name:

Password:

Security Question/Hint

Notes:

Website:

Email:

User Name:

Password:

Security Question/Hint

Notes:

M

Website:
Email:
User Name:
Password:
Security Question/Hint
Notes:

Website:
Email:
User Name:
Password:
Security Question/Hint
Notes:

Website:
Email:
User Name:
Password:
Security Question/Hint
Notes:

M

Website:
Email:
User Name:
Password:
Security Question/Hint
Notes:

Website:
Email:
User Name:
Password:
Security Question/Hint
Notes:

Website:
Email:
User Name:
Password:
Security Question/Hint
Notes:

M

Website:
Email:
User Name:
Password:
Security Question/Hint
Notes:

Website:
Email:
User Name:
Password:
Security Question/Hint
Notes:

Website:
Email:
User Name:
Password:
Security Question/Hint
Notes:

M

Website:
Email:
User Name:
Password:
Security Question/Hint
Notes:

Website:
Email:
User Name:
Password:
Security Question/Hint
Notes:

Website:
Email:
User Name:
Password:
Security Question/Hint
Notes:

N

Website:
Email:
User Name:
Password:
Security Question/Hint
Notes:

Website:
Email:
User Name:
Password:
Security Question/Hint
Notes:

Website:
Email:
User Name:
Password:
Security Question/Hint
Notes:

N

Website:
Email:
User Name:
Password:
Security Question/Hint
Notes:

Website:
Email:
User Name:
Password:
Security Question/Hint
Notes:

Website:
Email:
User Name:
Password:
Security Question/Hint
Notes:

N

Website:
Email:
User Name:
Password:
Security Question/Hint
Notes:

Website:
Email:
User Name:
Password:
Security Question/Hint
Notes:

Website:
Email:
User Name:
Password:
Security Question/Hint
Notes:

N

Website:
Email:
User Name:
Password:
Security Question/Hint
Notes:

Website:
Email:
User Name:
Password:
Security Question/Hint
Notes:

Website:
Email:
User Name:
Password:
Security Question/Hint
Notes:

Website:
Email:
User Name:
Password:
Security Question/Hint
Notes:

Website:
Email:
User Name:
Password:
Security Question/Hint
Notes:

Website:
Email:
User Name:
Password:
Security Question/Hint
Notes:

O

Website:
Email:
User Name:
Password:
Security Question/Hint
Notes:

Website:
Email:
User Name:
Password:
Security Question/Hint
Notes:

Website:
Email:
User Name:
Password:
Security Question/Hint
Notes:

Website:
Email:
User Name:
Password:
Security Question/Hint
Notes:

Website:
Email:
User Name:
Password:
Security Question/Hint
Notes:

Website:
Email:
User Name:
Password:
Security Question/Hint
Notes:

O

Website:
Email:
User Name:
Password:
Security Question/Hint
Notes:

Website:
Email:
User Name:
Password:
Security Question/Hint
Notes:

Website:
Email:
User Name:
Password:
Security Question/Hint
Notes:

P

Website:
Email:
User Name:
Password:
Security Question/Hint
Notes:

Website:
Email:
User Name:
Password:
Security Question/Hint
Notes:

Website:
Email:
User Name:
Password:
Security Question/Hint
Notes:

P

Website:
Email:
User Name:
Password:
Security Question/Hint
Notes:

Website:
Email:
User Name:
Password:
Security Question/Hint
Notes:

Website:
Email:
User Name:
Password:
Security Question/Hint
Notes:

P

Website:
Email:
User Name:
Password:
Security Question/Hint
Notes:

Website:
Email:
User Name:
Password:
Security Question/Hint
Notes:

Website:
Email:
User Name:
Password:
Security Question/Hint
Notes:

P

Website:
Email:
User Name:
Password:
Security Question/Hint
Notes:

Website:
Email:
User Name:
Password:
Security Question/Hint
Notes:

Website:
Email:
User Name:
Password:
Security Question/Hint
Notes:

Q

Website:
Email:
User Name:
Password:
Security Question/Hint
Notes:

Website:
Email:
User Name:
Password:
Security Question/Hint
Notes:

Website:
Email:
User Name:
Password:
Security Question/Hint
Notes:

Q

Website:
Email:
User Name:
Password:
Security Question/Hint
Notes:

Website:
Email:
User Name:
Password:
Security Question/Hint
Notes:

Website:
Email:
User Name:
Password:
Security Question/Hint
Notes:

Website:
Email:
User Name:
Password:
Security Question/Hint
Notes:

Website:
Email:
User Name:
Password:
Security Question/Hint
Notes:

Website:
Email:
User Name:
Password:
Security Question/Hint
Notes:

Q

Website:
Email:
User Name:
Password:
Security Question/Hint
Notes:

Website:
Email:
User Name:
Password:
Security Question/Hint
Notes:

Website:
Email:
User Name:
Password:
Security Question/Hint
Notes:

R

Website:
Email:
User Name:
Password:
Security Question/Hint
Notes:

Website:
Email:
User Name:
Password:
Security Question/Hint
Notes:

Website:
Email:
User Name:
Password:
Security Question/Hint
Notes:

R

Website:
Email:
User Name:
Password:

Security Question/Hint

Notes:

Website:
Email:
User Name:
Password:

Security Question/Hint

Notes:

Website:
Email:
User Name:
Password:

Security Question/Hint

Notes:

R

Website:
Email:
User Name:
Password:
Security Question/Hint
Notes:

Website:
Email:
User Name:
Password:
Security Question/Hint
Notes:

Website:
Email:
User Name:
Password:
Security Question/Hint
Notes:

R

Website:
Email:
User Name:
Password:
Security Question/Hint
Notes:

Website:
Email:
User Name:
Password:
Security Question/Hint
Notes:

Website:
Email:
User Name:
Password:
Security Question/Hint
Notes:

S

Website:
Email:
User Name:
Password:
Security Question/Hint
Notes:

Website:
Email:
User Name:
Password:
Security Question/Hint
Notes:

Website:
Email:
User Name:
Password:
Security Question/Hint
Notes:

S

Website:
Email:
User Name:
Password:
Security Question/Hint
Notes:

Website:
Email:
User Name:
Password:
Security Question/Hint
Notes:

Website:
Email:
User Name:
Password:
Security Question/Hint
Notes:

S

Website:
Email:
User Name:
Password:
Security Question/Hint
Notes:

Website:
Email:
User Name:
Password:
Security Question/Hint
Notes:

Website:
Email:
User Name:
Password:
Security Question/Hint
Notes:

S

Website:
Email:
User Name:
Password:
Security Question/Hint
Notes:

Website:
Email:
User Name:
Password:
Security Question/Hint
Notes:

Website:
Email:
User Name:
Password:
Security Question/Hint
Notes:

T

Website:
Email:
User Name:
Password:
Security Question/Hint
Notes:

Website:
Email:
User Name:
Password:
Security Question/Hint
Notes:

Website:
Email:
User Name:
Password:
Security Question/Hint
Notes:

T

Website:
Email:
User Name:
Password:
Security Question/Hint
Notes:

Website:
Email:
User Name:
Password:
Security Question/Hint
Notes:

Website:
Email:
User Name:
Password:
Security Question/Hint
Notes:

T

Website:
Email:
User Name:
Password:
Security Question/Hint
Notes:

Website:
Email:
User Name:
Password:
Security Question/Hint
Notes:

Website:
Email:
User Name:
Password:
Security Question/Hint
Notes:

T

Website:
Email:
User Name:
Password:
Security Question/Hint
Notes:

Website:
Email:
User Name:
Password:
Security Question/Hint
Notes:

Website:
Email:
User Name:
Password:
Security Question/Hint
Notes:

U

Website:
Email:
User Name:
Password:
Security Question/Hint
Notes:

Website:
Email:
User Name:
Password:
Security Question/Hint
Notes:

Website:
Email:
User Name:
Password:
Security Question/Hint
Notes:

U

Website:
Email:
User Name:
Password:
Security Question/Hint
Notes:

Website:
Email:
User Name:
Password:
Security Question/Hint
Notes:

Website:
Email:
User Name:
Password:
Security Question/Hint
Notes:

U

Website:
Email:
User Name:
Password:
Security Question/Hint
Notes:

Website:
Email:
User Name:
Password:
Security Question/Hint
Notes:

Website:
Email:
User Name:
Password:
Security Question/Hint
Notes:

U

Website:
Email:
User Name:
Password:
Security Question/Hint
Notes:

Website:
Email:
User Name:
Password:
Security Question/Hint
Notes:

Website:
Email:
User Name:
Password:
Security Question/Hint
Notes:

V

Website:
Email:
User Name:
Password:
Security Question/Hint
Notes:

Website:
Email:
User Name:
Password:
Security Question/Hint
Notes:

Website:
Email:
User Name:
Password:
Security Question/Hint
Notes:

V

Website:
Email:
User Name:
Password:
Security Question/Hint
Notes:

Website:
Email:
User Name:
Password:
Security Question/Hint
Notes:

Website:
Email:
User Name:
Password:
Security Question/Hint
Notes:

V

Website:
Email:
User Name:
Password:
Security Question/Hint
Notes:

Website:
Email:
User Name:
Password:
Security Question/Hint
Notes:

Website:
Email:
User Name:
Password:
Security Question/Hint
Notes:

V

Website:
Email:
User Name:
Password:
Security Question/Hint
Notes:

Website:
Email:
User Name:
Password:
Security Question/Hint
Notes:

Website:
Email:
User Name:
Password:
Security Question/Hint
Notes:

W

Website:
Email:
User Name:
Password:
Security Question/Hint
Notes:

Website:
Email:
User Name:
Password:
Security Question/Hint
Notes:

Website:
Email:
User Name:
Password:
Security Question/Hint
Notes:

W

Website:
Email:
User Name:
Password:
Security Question/Hint
Notes:

Website:
Email:
User Name:
Password:
Security Question/Hint
Notes:

Website:
Email:
User Name:
Password:
Security Question/Hint
Notes:

W

Website:
Email:
User Name:
Password:
Security Question/Hint
Notes:

Website:
Email:
User Name:
Password:
Security Question/Hint
Notes:

Website:
Email:
User Name:
Password:
Security Question/Hint
Notes:

W

Website:
Email:
User Name:
Password:
Security Question/Hint
Notes:

Website:
Email:
User Name:
Password:
Security Question/Hint
Notes:

Website:
Email:
User Name:
Password:
Security Question/Hint
Notes:

X

Website:
Email:
User Name:
Password:
Security Question/Hint
Notes:

Website:
Email:
User Name:
Password:
Security Question/Hint
Notes:

Website:
Email:
User Name:
Password:
Security Question/Hint
Notes:

X

Website:
Email:
User Name:
Password:
Security Question/Hint
Notes:

Website:
Email:
User Name:
Password:
Security Question/Hint
Notes:

Website:
Email:
User Name:
Password:
Security Question/Hint
Notes:

X

Website:
Email:
User Name:
Password:
Security Question/Hint
Notes:

Website:
Email:
User Name:
Password:
Security Question/Hint
Notes:

Website:
Email:
User Name:
Password:
Security Question/Hint
Notes:

X

Website:
Email:
User Name:
Password:
Security Question/Hint
Notes:

Website:
Email:
User Name:
Password:
Security Question/Hint
Notes:

Website:
Email:
User Name:
Password:
Security Question/Hint
Notes:

Y

Website:
Email:
User Name:
Password:
Security Question/Hint
Notes:

Website:
Email:
User Name:
Password:
Security Question/Hint
Notes:

Website:
Email:
User Name:
Password:
Security Question/Hint
Notes:

Y

Website:
Email:
User Name:
Password:
Security Question/Hint
Notes:

Website:
Email:
User Name:
Password:
Security Question/Hint
Notes:

Website:
Email:
User Name:
Password:
Security Question/Hint
Notes:

Y

Website:
Email:
User Name:
Password:
Security Question/Hint
Notes:

Website:
Email:
User Name:
Password:
Security Question/Hint
Notes:

Website:
Email:
User Name:
Password:
Security Question/Hint
Notes:

Y

Website:
Email:
User Name:
Password:
Security Question/Hint
Notes:

Website:
Email:
User Name:
Password:
Security Question/Hint
Notes:

Website:
Email:
User Name:
Password:
Security Question/Hint
Notes:

Z

Website:
Email:
User Name:
Password:
Security Question/Hint
Notes:

Website:
Email:
User Name:
Password:
Security Question/Hint
Notes:

Website:
Email:
User Name:
Password:
Security Question/Hint
Notes:

Z

Website:
Email:
User Name:
Password:
Security Question/Hint
Notes:

Website:
Email:
User Name:
Password:
Security Question/Hint
Notes:

Website:
Email:
User Name:
Password:
Security Question/Hint
Notes:

Z

Website:
Email:
User Name:
Password:
Security Question/Hint
Notes:

Website:
Email:
User Name:
Password:
Security Question/Hint
Notes:

Website:
Email:
User Name:
Password:
Security Question/Hint
Notes:

Z

Website:
Email:
User Name:
Password:
Security Question/Hint
Notes:

Website:
Email:
User Name:
Password:
Security Question/Hint
Notes:

Website:
Email:
User Name:
Password:
Security Question/Hint
Notes:

≪ NOTES ≫

NOTES

≪ NOTES ≫

NOTES

≪ NOTES ≫

≪ NOTES ≫

Made in the USA
Monee, IL
04 November 2026

67386648R00066